To Celia
who does so much
the regimental museum

CW01082362

ESSAYS ON FAMOUS FIGURES
OF
BRECON CATHEDRAL

By

Jonathan Morgan

The right of Jonathan Morgan to be identified as the author of this work has been asserted by him in accordance with the Copyright, Designs and Patents Act, 1988.

Copyright ©2021 Jonathan Morgan.

ISBN 978-1-8384289-3-8

All rights reserved. No part of this publication may be reproduced, stored in retrieval system or transmitted in any form or by any means electronic, mechanical, photocopying, recording or otherwise, without the prior permission of the publisher, except in the case of brief quotations embodied in critical articles and reviews.

Published in the United Kingdom in 2021 by
Cambria Publishing Ltd, Wales, United Kingdom.
Website: www.cambriabooks.co.uk

Illustrations by Robert Macdonald RWSW (President), MA (RCA), Diop.LCSAD.

DEDICATION

This book is dedicated to Brecon Cathedral, which has given the author many profound moments of meditation and has alerted his interest in the deep roots of this spiritual home.

A great thank you to the Veterans Foundation without whose help the book could not have been written.

The Veterans' Foundation is one of the country's fastest-growing military charities and we are proud to work with hundreds of smaller charities and charitable organisations across UK that share our passion: to provide a better life for our Armed Forces family who are in need (our beneficiaries).

We help our partner organisations by supporting them to deliver life-changing projects through our grant award scheme.

Many amazing charities have significant financial constraints and the Veterans' Foundation exists to champion their causes and to help them effect their objectives.

We do this by funding projects and we also work with our partners to broadcast their initiatives so we can raise awareness of the challenges facing our armed forces community. We know those challenges can often impact on family members and our pledge is to also offer support for the dependents of those who have served their country.

The Veterans' Foundation has a unique story. We were formed in 2016 and we have grown quickly since then.

Our journey began by sharing the stories of our Armed Forces family on social media and this quickly escalated into a large, trusted community of friends and supporters. In just a few years we've engaged and interacted with millions of you, celebrating our Armed Forces and bringing hope of a better life to those in need of care and assistance.

Our supporters, you, are the heartbeat of the Veterans' Foundation and through your kind donations, fundraising events and by playing our popular Veterans' Lottery, challenges are being faced, overcome, and lives are changing for the better.

Thank you for your support.

THANKS AND ACKNOWLEDGEMENTS

FRANCES CHAFFEY for her secretarial skills; ROBERT MACDONALD for his illustrations; ALISON CROCKETT for her proof reading; and CHRIS AND ANNETTE THOMAS for their financial contribution and article.

GLYN MATHIAS for his article on the Cobbes in Brycheiniog; the late TONY BELL for his article in the same publication on The Camdens; KEN JONES on Captain Frederick Jones; and JOSEPHINE COPPING on Captain Maybery.

The Usk Valley Trust for their generous donation.

Simon Harpur for photographs of Brecon Cathedral.

ABOUT THE AUTHOR

Jonathan Morgan was educated at Christ College, Brecon, RMA Sandhurst, and Aberystwyth, Cardiff and Glamorgan Universities. He also taught at UWIC (now Cardiff Metropolitan) for nine years. Jonathan's father, the Rev. G Rex Morgan, Chaplain to the King's Royal Rifle Corps and Senior Housemaster at Christ College, Brecon, was a well-known prisoner-of-war and was on the dreadful 'Shoe Leather Express' March in Poland. It is interesting that Christ College former pupils won 23 MCs in the First World War.

Jonathan's was a great Welsh sporting family which included Guy Morgan, Captain of Cambridge University and Wales at rugby and Glamorgan at Cricket, and Dr. Teddy Morgan, Captain of Wales and the British Lions at rugby. Rex's cousin Guy (not the rugby player), was a Royal Navy Lieutenant and prisoner-of-war who wrote the well-known play *'Albert R.N'*, Jonathan's mother, Glenys, was the daughter of Captain T.L.Morgan, Adjutant of the 15th Welsh in the early part of the Great War.

As well as a sportsman himself, Jonathan is a 3rd Order Anglican Franciscan. He was invalided out of the Army with PTSD or related illness in 1980 and had served with the Royal Regiment of Wales as a Captain which included an horrific tour of Northern Ireland in the Ardoyne and Bone district of Belfast.

ABOUT THE ILLUSTRATOR

Robert Macdonald, an artist who lives near Brecon, is a past Chair of the Welsh Group, the senior association of professional artists in Wales, and President of the Royal Watercolour Society of Wales. He is a graduate of the Royal College of Art. Born in 1935, his childhood was shaped by the upheavals of the Second World War. After losing their home in a wartime bombing raid the Macdonalds emigrated to New Zealand in 1945. Robert did military service in the New Zealand Army.

He returned to Britain in 1958 and studied at the London Central School of Art. Since coming to live in Wales with his Welsh-born wife Annie he has been inspired by the Welsh landscape and mythology.

CONTENTS

FOREWORD

'Essays on Famous Figures of Brecon Cathedral' is a rich collection of interesting stories and historical facts about people and events that have connections and have shaped the town and Cathedral of Brecon. Jonathan draws imaginatively on the Cathedral's memorials, effigies, building, artifacts, and graves, to convey a tapestry of Brecon's history through the compilation of interesting figures and artifacts.

Through the pages of the book, you will learn fascinating historical facts and stories that will be helpful to the inquiring visitor or tourist, resident of the town, or Cathedral tour guide.

You will find in this book a list of distinguished significant people with their human endeavours of gallantry, heroism, and philanthropic contributions to Brecon. The essays showcase Brecon as a place that have known ordinary and great people who have contributed to the military, agricultural, artistic, ecclesiastical, educational, architectural, musical, and legal professions. Traversing centuries to the present day, Jonathan impressively draws on the rich artifacts of the Cathedral's paintings, gates and graves, memorials, architecture, and stained-glass windows. each revealing Brecon's rich heritage, history, and culture, and how people past and present have contributed to its richness.

Finally, I welcome Jonathan's invitation to write this foreword. But the foreword would not be complete without me mentioning someone who is omitted in the book who also contributes to Brecon and the Cathedral today. And so, it is fitting that I give credit to Jonathan for his daily commitment to Brecon, the Cathedral, and his thoughtful and wise encouragement and commitment to the life, ministry, and mission of the Cathedral, particularly to me as the Dean. He is a presence and gift to Brecon and the Cathedral who continues to daily enrich the lives of many with wisdom, faith, and knowledge.

As Jonathan's book bears witness to the examples of those who have gone before us, may those who live and work in Brecon and the Cathedral continue to be committed custodians of a great history and heritage for this and future generations.

The Very Reverend Dr Paul Shackerley

Dean of Brecon

THE CELTIC SAINTS

With the Norman knights on the windows in the St Keyne's chapel, are images of Celtic saints, and there is a little evidence that there may have been a Celtic church on this site before the Norman church.

St.Illtyd

As for the saints, Illtyd was a native of Brittany, and was called by the Welsh authorities 'The Knight' since he was probably engaged in a military career for some time. He served in the court of Saul, King of Morganwg. One day, the king was out hunting in the Vale of Glamorgan, when, feeling hungry and being near Llancarfan, he ordered his men to go to St Cadoc's Abbey and take what was required for their meal.

The first community there, founded by Illtyd, was one in which the married people lived together, as was usual in Celtic communities of the first period; probably the transition to the second stage was marked by the settlement at Llantwit Major.

St.Cadoc

There are various stories about St Illtyd's miracles, including his quarrel with the local landowner. According to legend, the superintendent of the local landowner was cursed by the saint; thereupon he melted down into a lump of beeswax. St Illtyd also paid a visit to Brittany, and during a time of famine was able to send corn from Wales for the relief of the starving people.

St Keyne, or St Cenau, was reputed to have been the daughter of Brychan, King of Brecknock. She forsook her native country and found some deserted places where she could find time for prayer and contemplation. So, having crossed the Severn, she arrived in a wooded country and obtained permission from the Prince of that region to settle there. It was full of serpents and snakes, and he thought she had no chance of living there but she prayed, and the serpents were turned into stone. She eventually went to Cornwall, before returning to Llangenny in Abergavenny, where she brought forth a miraculous spring. The day of her death was highlighted by a column of fire, and two angels announced that they would introduce her to 'The Kingdom of my Father'.

St.Alud

Also in the windows of the Keyne's Chapel is St Cadoc who lived in a monastery in Caerwent, and later founded a monastery at Llancarfan. Here, also, is the virgin martyr, St Alud. She is depicted near her cell in the Brecon Beacons and at her feet is the stream which gushed from the rocks on Slwch Tump at her martyrdom. Brychan is also depicted, and to his right is St Cynog, who founded nearby places of worship at Defynnog, Battle and Ystradgynlais, and was killed by the Saxons near Merthyr Cynog.

This chapel later became a shrine for shoemakers, or cordwainers. The patron saint of shoemakers was St Crispin, and it was on his day, 25th October, that the Battle of Agincourt took place in 1415 where about 160 archers had gone from Brecon to fight in the battle. So this may well be the link with the cordwainers.

Annually, from 1936 to 1995, the British Boot and Shoe Federation processed from the Guildhall for their service here.

The other person of note portrayed on the windows is Cyril Flower, who became Lord Battersea. In 1880, he became Liberal MP for Brecon, supported by his wife's fortune, and sponsored the windows in the chapel.

THE NORMAN LORDS

Giles de Brecon

There is no doubt that the Normans were greedy, and Bernard de Neufmarche was a member of a prominent Norman family who came across with William I. He advanced with his knights towards Brecon, where the Gaer was the most westerly northern outpost, guarding the routes along the Norman ways leading to the north and west. With the arrival of Rhys ap Tewdwr, who had in the meantime been engaged in quelling Welsh rivals, the Norman base was subject to a considerable Welsh attack, but thanks to their remarkable discipline, the rather disorganised and wild Welsh attack was defeated. Rhys was killed, and with his death, Welsh resistance in Brycheiniog was overcome.

Humphries de Bohun

On the north side of the Usk, Bernard built a strong castle on an eminence and built his residence with whatever materials were worth carrying or preserving. He removed materials from the old town and employed these in the erection of his new fortress and in building habitations for his followers and dependents. Among his knights were Sir Reginald Awbrey, to whom he gave the manors of Slwch and Abercynrig, and whose descendants' memorial survives in the Hafod Chapel in Brecon Cathedral. Also to Sir John Skull he gave the manors of Bolgoed and Crai.

He, again, has a memorial given to the Cathedral in the form of a chair, the money having been raised by his American descendants.

Brecon became the spiritual centre of the lordship, by the grant of the Church of St John, built by Bernard on the outskirts of the north wall of the castle as a cell to Battle Abbey. A grant was made at the suggestion of Roger, a monk of Battle, then officiating as chaplain to the castle. In conjunction with Walter, a fellow monk, Roger began to erect monastic buildings alongside the church. After Bernard's death, his land eventually became part of the de Braose lands, a region of considerable extent in the middle march. However, the hostility of William de Braose towards his Welsh subjects brought in its train much bitterness, and although William, after 1195, was a favourite of the crown, he later suffered a rapid downfall in royal favour, partly because he failed to discharge his debts to the crown. Reginald de Braose, who became Lord of Brecon, died in 1228 and is said to have been buried on the south side of the high altar.

Brecon Cathedral, especially the presbytery and crossing, was rebuilt in the early 13th century. The nave was altered, and the north transept built or rebuilt during the late 13th and early 14th centuries and the south transept was added later in the 14th century. Of the Norman Church, built for the repose of the soul of William the Conqueror, the only remains are the font and the north and south walls in the nave. The present church was begun in the early part of the 13th century, at the time of Giles de Braose, Bishop of Hereford. Humphrey de Bohun inherited the earldoms of Hereford and Essex, and part of Brecon became part of his domain. During de Braose's time as lord, the tower was started, although it took 200 years to complete. This is why de Braose is seen to carry a tower in the stained glass window portrait. Thus it was the Normans who were primarily responsible for the priory at Brecon, which later became Brecon Cathedral. They employed many of their own masons and it was their advancement in building techniques, as well as their weapons and armoured protection which established them in this area as the conquerors of the Welsh.

The stained glass windows in St Keyne's window reflect the prominence of the Normans, and also of the Dukes of Buckingham, of whom we shall hear more in the next chapter.

THE DUKES OF BUCKINGHAM

Dukes of Buckingham

When Richard III came to the throne, Duke Henry of Buckingham gave his support to the new king, which resulted in many high offices being granted to him. By October 1483 he had been made Chief Justice of north and south Wales for life, but had also obtained the Constableship, Stewardship and Receiver Generalship of all the crown lands there. Orders were sent out enabling him to take possession of castles and armaments throughout Wales. This made it very hard to understand Buckingham's sudden decision to join forces with his aunt, Lady Margaret

Beaufort and a group of disgruntled Yorkists, in a rebellion against the king. Sir Thomas More believed that the persuasive influence of Bishop Morton, then a prisoner in Brecon Castle, was instrumental in motivating the rebellion which rapidly collapsed, partly due to so few of his tenants taking part in the rising.

Buckingham then marched from Brecon, but many of his men did not want to fight. He made no appeal to Welsh national sentiment, and he made many enemies, especially the Vaughans and William Herbert. Thus he went into hiding, but was betrayed by one of his own servants, and was summarily executed without trial at Salisbury on 2nd November, 1483. The Duke's five year old son, Henry, was taken to safety, and when Henry VII assumed the throne, he restored some of the Buckingham estates. After Henry VII's death, the 3rd Duke of Buckingham tried to recover the constableship of England for himself and his descendants as the heirs of Humphrey de Bohun, Earl of Hereford, who was one of the marcher lords. He won his claim to be confirmed Constable of England, but this did not favour him with Henry VIII as he was deemed to be a possible rival to the king. Duke Edward went on to criticise Cardinal Wolsey's foreign policy, which did not endear him to Henry's court at the time. He was intolerant, and often wantonly vindictive towards his servants, some of whom reported to Wolsey on his indiscretions.

Edward, Duke of Buckingham, died because his pride and ambition made it impossible for him to accept the passive role of satellite and courtier which had also been forced on so many of his peers. He had failed to convince the king that his wealth, territorial power and royal blood did not constitute a grave threat to the established order, and the penalty was death. In retrospect, the succession of blunders occasioned by Duke Edward's inability to appreciate the delicacy of his position can be seen to have led directly to his execution on Tower Hill. Henry VIII then kept the Duke's Welsh marcher lordships in his own hands and used the rest of the English estates for purposes of patronage.

The first duke, Humphrey, had always been jealous of Henry VII's use of his patronage, often bypassing the duke. So there had been a tradition of the Buckinghams not being comfortable with their kings. After the execution of Edward, Duke of Buckingham, Brecon reverted to the hands of the king, and it is interesting that the Brecon coat of arms carries the ducal ermine robe of the Buckinghams. The Buckinghams are the last of the lords to be shown in St Keyne's Chapel.

THE CHURCH MICE

On the screen as you come out of the St Keynes Chapel there is a mouse carved. Famous for his mice, Robert 'Mouseman' Thompson who lived from 7th May 1876 - 8th December 1955 was a British furniture maker. He was born and lived in Kilburn, North Yorkshire, where he set up a business manufacturing oak furniture which featured a carved mouse on almost every piece. It is claimed that the mouse motif came about accidentally in 1919 following a conversation about being, 'As poor as a church mouse' which took place between Thompson and one of his colleagues during the carving of a cornice for a screen. This chance remark led to him carving a mouse and this remained part of his work from this point onwards.

Thompson was part of the 1920s revival of craftsmanship inspired by the arts and crafts movement led by William Morris, John Ruskin and Thomas Carlisle. He obviously worked on this screen in the Cathedral. That particular mouse has never been found, but it has continued as a trademark of quality and dedication to craftsmen ever since. We wonder if the Cathedral one is the original?

Thompson Carving on the Corvizers screen, St Keyne's chapel

In one of the windows of St Keyne's Chapel is St Cadoc. He is accompanied by a white mouse. He was setting up his monastery and the disciples that he gathered around him were actually starving and a rather plump mouse came along, sat on his desk and dropped a corn, a small wheat corn which the saint quickly ate. Then the mouse went away, brought another and dropped it in the same place.

St Cadoc thought, 'Why is this mouse so well fed? He tied a piece of cotton thread to the mouse's tail and followed the string. He then came upon a sort of cabin in which was a stash of corn, so the monks didn't starve.

THE WELSH ARCHERS IN THE 100 YEARS WAR

Welsh Archers

At the entrance to the Chapel of St Keyne is a separated effigy of one of the Gam family. Their ancestor, Sir Dafydd Gam, played an important part in the Battle of Agincourt, commanding a company of the Welsh archers. There is a list of the archers who came from Brecknockshire on a table in the south aisle. Also, on the top window of the south transept, there is a stained glass window featuring Sir Roger Vaughan who also helped to lead the Welsh archers at Agincourt.

Edward I, after his conquest of Wales found that he could recruit many Welshmen as soldiers for his frequent wars in Scotland and France. The speciality of the Welsh was their outstanding skill as archers. They used the longbow better than anyone else at this time.

Welsh archers served under Edward I at the battle of Falkirk, one of the major battles in the First War of Scottish Independence, as early as 1298, and, from then onwards, were found in large numbers in the English armies of the 14th century.

There was a preponderance of Welsh archers at the battles of Crecy in 1346 and Poitiers in 1456. The Red Dragon of Cadwallader, a Welsh hero of the 7th century became the recognised emblem of the Welsh.

When the Black Prince was thrown from his horse at Crecy, it was the dragon banner of Wales that was flung over him in protection while his enemies were beaten off. It was probably at Crecy that the leek became the Welshman's special badge when the Welsh men plucked leeks and wore them in their helmets, although this tradition is said to have gone back even as far as St David's time.

The green and white of the Welsh banner may reflect the colour of the leek, and certainly it was associated with the royal colours of Wales. Prince Llewelyn was said to have been married in green and white. The colour was also associated with Cheshire, probably in the first uniforms of the Black Prince's archers, as he was also Earl of Chester.

It is most interesting that the board that was in Brecon Cathedral's Heritage Centre, recording the names of approximately 160 archers who went from the environs of Brecon to fight at Agincourt, is now in the south aisle of the cathedral. The authenticity of the names is not questionable; they do fit in with the names recorded in *The Roll of Agincourt*. Although I have not checked every name, there is enough similarity to consider the board accurate. We do not know where the information came from but we suspect at one time it was in some sort of museum in America, was transferred to the Brecon Museum and thence to the Heritage Centre and the south aisle of the Cathedral.

The archers from Wales carried the longbow, which was equal to the height of a man, and used it with deadly accuracy which made them famous throughout Europe. There is certainly some foundation in the story that the longbow had originally come out of Wales. The Welsh bowmen of the Black Prince helped to win many battles, were considered highly disciplined, and were some of the first infantry in Europe to wear uniform, the green and white colours of Wales, as previously mentioned.

Their dress was most interesting: they wore helmets and caps made of boiled leather and sleeveless garments made of quilted coarse linen which resembled the padding on a modern fencing jacket. When in action, the shirt sleeves would be rolled up and on the left forearm would be the leather brace, which was about five inches long, to take the impact of the bow string. They wore coarse homespun breeches gathered at the knee and soft leather jackboots of the kind we associate with Russian peasants (minus high heels). A small round target or shield was carried on the left side of the sword and a mace was often carried as a small side arm. Hanging from the belt, in front, to the right, was a small pouch for the archer's wax and odds and ends. Arrows were carried in sheaves of about 12, loosely bound, and slung on the back or thrust through the belt. During a battle further ammunition was supplied by special runners.

Archers also carried a pole or palisade, a stake about eleven feet long and sharpened at both ends. These were set up fairly close together with one end embedded in the ground and the other pointing outward at about the height of a horse's chest, which formed a good protection against cavalry charges. There would be no issued uniform, although, certainly earlier in the French wars, the Welsh would wear the green and white colours. It is probable that all the troops in the King's army at Agincourt wore on their back and chest the red cross of St George on a white field.

I have a letter from reader James Travers, National Archives, which gives a fascinating account of the archers at Agincourt, as follows:

'There were certainly both Welsh and English archers present at Agincourt but to establish relative numbers from the surviving documents is problematic. To begin with the term 'archer' as it appears in early fifteenth century musters did not necessarily denote a longbowman. 'Archer' simply distinguished soldiers paid at a certain rate from men at arms paid at another. Their weapons varied.

The surviving retinue rolls only gave a partial view of the composition of Henry's force that would have included Irish and Burgundians as well as English and Welsh. Welsh archers are known, from a variety of sources, to have joined the expedition to France.

Among the most distinguished of these were Roger Vaughan of Bredwardine; Watkin Lloyd of the Lordship of Brecknock; and the renowned David Llewelyn, better known as Dafydd Gam.

Such lists of archers as we have suggest a preponderance of English names, but this raises further questions about rendering Welsh patronyms in official documents and the greater likelihood of certain social groups being more recorded than others.'

Wales has a long tradition of archery going back to the mythological figure Gwrnerth Ergydlym, or Powerful Sharpshot, who reputedly slew the largest boar in Britain with an arrow of straw.

In Welsh tradition, messengers calling warriors to battle rode through the land waving a strung bow, while the return of peace was announced by the same, unstrung. The earliest bow found in Britain is dated 2690 BC. Is this a Celtic bow? It is over six feet long, a powerful yew, bow bound with leather thongs in an intricate criss-cross pattern, and a good deal taller than the archer who shot it!

A longbow is made of wood, as opposed to those composite bows found in other parts of the world, and its length is at least equal to the height of the user and may even be a little more. Its width and thickness are nearly equal and in this it contrasts with the flat bow where the width is appreciably greater than its thickness.

From the military point of view, the advantage of the longbow is its ability to shoot a heavy arrow to an adequate range, in the order of 200 yards. Weight is needed in the shaft to achieve the penetration of mail and armour.

Records suggest that the most popular wood for bows at the time was the local wych or wild elm. However, the qualities of the yew, particularly from trees growing on harsh upland ground, was found to be superior. The best yew grows under hard conditions where slow growth gives the wood a close grain. Bows are made from the main trunk of the tree and not from the branches, unless they are very large. In bow manufacture a combination of the outer sapwood and the inner heartwood is essential.

The appropriate yews were felled between December and February when sap levels are down and were then seasoned in kitchens, suspended high up with the hams in the smoke blackened beams. Another important source of good yew for bow making was the Spanish peninsula and a thriving trade developed with medieval Wales. Other woods such as ash were popular with the Welsh archers. The idea that yews were planted in churchyards to provide wood for bows is a popular fallacy. They were planted as a sombre evergreen, suitable for the solemnity of such places.

Archery was an essential part of a man's life. From an early age, boys were encouraged to shoot and would have grown up in a society where proficiency with the bow was a skill at which to shine. It has interested our national psyche; even the notorious two fingered salute, offensive today, represented little more than a gesture of defiance in the face of the enemy, who sliced off the first two fingers of any captured bowmen.

Having looked at the longbow and the archers; also having looked at the composition of the British force at Agincourt, we ought perhaps to look more closely at the battle.

It took place on 25th October 1415 on St Crispin's Day. Henry V's army of 9,000 men defeated a French army of at least four times that number. It was David Gam, the Welsh squire, who had raised a body of men from Breconshire, who was sent on the eve of the battle by the King to explore the numbers of the enemy. He returned to make the well- known answer: 'Enough to be taken prisoners and enough to run away'.

Several attacks were made by the French, some of them almost succeeding in overrunning the King's kinsman Walter Llwyd. At that very moment the archers, using their axes or swords, were slaughtered or taken prisoner to a man.

A prominent soldier was the afore mentioned David Gam, and despite popular myth, there was no evidence that he was knighted on the field. He was the man who at Owain Glyndwr's first parliament at Machynlleth attempted to kill the Welsh patriot and broke his pledge to Glyndwr time after time.

The Welsh quisling (a traitor who collaborates with an enemy force occupying his country) slew his kinsman, Richard Fawr, Lord of Slwch, in the High Street of Brecon and this caused him to flee from Wales and seek service with Harry of Monmouth. We are not sure if he was called Gam because he squinted or because his legs were crooked. He was killed at Agincourt and probably buried there, although, it is rumoured that many of his descendants were buried under the choir in the Chapel of Christ College, Brecon and we have a memorial to two of his descendants in Brecon Cathedral.

His family once lived in Newton Farm on the edge of Llanfaes in Brecon and there are still many of the Games family about in the area. His descendants in the male line eventually adopted the surname Games. They were among the most prominent patrons of Welsh poetry in the fifteenth century. Gwladys, Dafydd Gam's daughter, married successively Sir Roger Vaughan of Tretower, and Sir William ap Thomas of Raglan. Her son, by the latter marriage, was William, the first Herbert, Earl of Pembroke. The author has neglected to put William Herbert in his book of 'Famous Figures of Christ College Brecon', for the former was educated there up until the age of 14 and is probably its most illustrious pupil. I believe Sir Roger Vaughan, Gam's son-in-law, who also fought at Agincourt, was killed; his image is in the top stained glass window of the south transept in the Cathedral. There is little else I can find out about him except that he was of the well-connected Vaughan family.

Among the Welsh at Agincourt, Harry of Monmouth, if Shakespeare is to be believed, counted himself as one of them, for to Fluellen's remark that, 'Welshmen did good service in a garden where Leeke did grow, wearing leeks in their Monmouth caps', the King replies, 'I wear it for a memorable honour for I am Welsh, you know, good countryman'.

Bibliography:

Spencer, J., *The Welsh Archer* (Warbow Wales, the home of the Welsh medieval longbow).

Sumption, J*., The Hundred years War* (Faber&Faber, 1990).

Sumption, J*., The Hundred Years War, Trial by Fire* (Faber&Faber,2011).

Shakespeare and Wales, ed. W. Maley and P. Schwyzer (Ashgate Publishing, England 2010).

DR THOMAS COKE

Thomas Coke

Just on the outside of St Keyne's Chapel on the north wall, is a memorial to Dr Thomas Coke. A man whose 150th anniversary was celebrated in 1964, Thomas Coke was born in 1747. When he matured he was only five feet one inch tall and had a tendency to put on weight, but he was a live wire who started off as an

Anglican, but after meeting John Wesley in August 1776, turned his back on the Church of England.

The year 1784 was a momentous one both for Methodism and for Thomas Coke, the young man from Christ College who had studied jurisprudence at Jesus College Oxford. That year also saw the culmination of his service as Wesley's administrative assistant in the drafting of the Deed of Declaration which gave legal status to the Methodist Conference and ensured the continuance of Methodism after its founder's death. Coke engaged in a bewildering number and variety of activities, continuing to be involved in the affairs of the British connection, but at the same time he was superintendent of the world mission of the Church, to which he was devoted, and a bishop David of the Methodist Episcopal Church of America. After a huge amount of work with Methodism, especially associated with the mission in America, he eventually died on a sea trip in May 1814. He was a great man.

DAVID GRIFFITHS

Along the wall from Coke's memorial is the memorial to headmaster David Griffith, the longest serving headmaster of Christ College, from 1758 – 1801. His time was notable for the number of pupils who achieved eminence. The school produced a group of Welsh-speaking nonconformists, a paradox, given the terms and intentions of the Founder's Charter. Thomas Price and John Hughes were prominent in the campaign to revive interest in the Welsh language and its literature. The former was a friend of Lady Llanover, whose husband 'Big Ben', Benjamin Hall, was later to be important in refounding the school in the 1850s. We have already talked about Thomas Coke. Another notable figure, Wales's best known landscape painter of the time, was Thomas Jones of Pencerrig.

Christ College chapel has a memorial to Theophilus Jones, whose history of his native county is indispensable to all modern researchers. Jones recorded the great respect in which he held Griffiths as a teacher.

RICHARD AVELINE MAYBERY

Richard Maybery

On the west wall of Brecon Cathedral, Richard Aveline Maybery, Jan 4th 1895 - 17th Dec 1917, is remembered; his name is up on the memorial there. The Mayberys have also been associated with the Priory since 1753, when a Thomas Maybery bought the furnace and forge in the Priory Groves and gave it to his son John, the ironmaster, who lived in the tower of the priory with his wife Ann. Richard's father was Henry Maybery, who was born at Ely Cottage, near the Bishop's Palace, who, on his mother's side, was the grandson of Joseph Richard Cobb and the great grandson of Parry de Winton. Before 1912, Richard Maybery was sent off to school, first to Connaught House in Weybridge, and then on to Wellington College in Berkshire. From Wellington, he won a prize cadetship to Sandhurst, passing out fifth and winning first prize for field engineering, and for tactics and strategy. He was also extremely good at all sports. In 1912, he was best man at his sister's wedding, when she married Hugh Griffith Coke Fowler of the 24th Regiment of foot. The reception was held on the tennis court where a long marquee led from the cathedral to the priory.

On 17th September 1913, he was commissioned as a 2nd lieutenant in the 21st Empress of India Lancers and was sent out to India where he was posted to Rawalpindi and the Sea Squadron fighting against the Mohnends on the northwest frontier. At the outbreak of war, he was promoted to lieutenant on the 31st October 1914. On 15th September 1915 Richard was wounded at the Charge of Shabkader while ADC to Brigadier General Crocker commanding the 1st Cavalry Brigade. During his rehabilitation, not being able to sit upon a horse, he became involved in observing for a unit of the Royal Flying Corps who were based nearby. He was eventually seconded to the RFC and appointed a flying officer on 10th October 1916. He was praised by the commander in chief in India for daring in low flying and bombing. In early 1917, he travelled to Egypt where he trained to be a pilot rather than an observer, passing first in all the examinations.

He returned to England, where he made a record flight in a scout machine. He was posted later in April to serve in 56 Squadron. The squadron moved to Vertgalant, France in April 1917, with the new Sopwith SE5 fighter scout planes. Richard shot down a German aircraft on his first patrol, which was a most unusual achievement. Six weeks later, he won his first Military Cross for attacking three aerodromes, dispersing mounted men, attacking goods trains, attacking, (single handed) large and hostile formations and setting a fine example by gallantry and determination. The squadron was later brought back from France to deal with German Gotha bombers attacking London. Aggressive and headstrong, Richard quickly accumulated a high victory tally, accounting for 21 enemy aircraft between

7th July and 19th December 1917.

He was awarded the Military Cross on 26th September and on 18th November was appointed a flight commander with the temporary rank of captain. His second Military Cross was awarded on 17th December. On 19th December he scored his 21st victory over Bourlon Wood, downing an Albatross DV, the German fighter aircraft which was after the squadron had returned to France. However, he was hit by anti-aircraft fire and crashed fatally 600 yards south of the village of Hayecourt.

He was buried, first where he fell, and later moved to Flesquires Hill Cemetery, Nord. He was awarded the MC for conspicuous gallantry and devotion to duty as leader of offensive patrols for three months, during which he personally destroyed nine enemy aeroplanes and drove down three out of control. On one occasion, having lost his patrol, he attacked a formation of eight enemy aeroplanes; one was seen to crash and two others went down out of control, completely breaking up the formation.

MAJOR DAVID PRICE

Anglo Dutch War

Just to the south of the west wall is a memorial to Major David Price, who was the eldest of five children born in Merthyr Cynog where his father had been curate since 1758. After his father died, David was offered a free place at Christ College, Brecon, where the headmaster, the Rev. David Griffith, had been his father's former rector. After performing well at classics, David was awarded a scholarship to Jesus College, Cambridge. But even on his way to university he spent extravagantly and despite coaxing money out of his relatives, he eventually found himself 'down and out'.

He saw an advertisement while he was at the Green Man and Still, an inn in Oxford Street, inviting all spirited young men to enlist in the East India Company, and thus volunteered as a private soldier. Whilst waiting to board the ship to India he was horrified by the atmosphere of debauchery and vice that prevailed at the port. Luckily, he was later rescued from the ranks, and supported as an officer cadet by the naval surgeon, Thomas Evans, a relation. Evans had previously rescued John Lloyd, another private soldier, in the same way. The latter then arranged for Price also to be accepted as an officer cadet.

When Price arrived in India he was attached to an infantry regiment and soon, in action off Ceylon, won some valuable prize money which he soon lost in the boredom of the rainy season at gambling, cards, and horses. Initially, he had some luck on the battlefield, two musket balls just missing him, but in 1791, during the Siege of Darwar, he was wounded and lost a leg.

He was now posted to various staff jobs and began to study Persian extensively. Thus he was appointed Persian translator to General James Stuart who took part in various campaigns in British India. David was promoted captain and in 1795 he achieved the important position of Judge Advocate of the Bombay Army. By 1799 he had secured such a reputation for integrity that he was appointed one of the seven prize agents during the campaign of the British East India Company to capture Seringpatam the capital of Tipu Sultan, ruler of Mysore. The official booty amounted to a huge sum, of which Price's share as prize agent was about £400,000. David Price was promoted to major in 1804 and then went home on leave, staying through the winter and spring with friends in London, and finally reached Brecon in June 1806 after an absence of twenty-nine years. He married, in April 1807, the daughter of a kinswoman and moved to Watton House where he lived for the rest of his life.

Having arrived in Brecon, after six months, Price resigned his commission. He subsequently held many public positions, including Bailiff of Brecon, magistrate, and deputy lieutenant of the county. He spent much of his time devoted to Oriental studies and wrote a series of books concerning Islamic and Indian culture and history; he was also recognised as one of the leading Oriental scholars of his day.

A renowned translator of Persian, in 1830 he received the Gold Medal of the Oriental Translation Committee. When he died on 16th December 1835, he was held in such high standing that all the gentry balls were cancelled. To some, however, he was the 'jolly old major' who, at social events, was 'drunk as usual'. He left seventy-three rare manuscripts to the Royal Asiatic Society, and to the sons of Walter Wilkins, a descendant of the De Wintons who served in the Honourable East India Company, and as MP for Radnor, he left £6,000.

SIR DAVID WILLIAMS

Sir David Williams and wife

Born circa 1536. Both this man's effigy, and that of his wife, are just to the right of the choir's entrance. Although he was of relatively humble origins, he preferred to tell friends that he was of the same house as the Lord Williams of Thame. He was admitted to the Middle Temple in 1568, and called to the Bar in 1578, after which he seems to have practised chiefly in South Wales where he acquired the Priory of St John in Brecon and in 1600, a house at Gwernyfed, near Hay on Wye. He became a justice of the peace for Brecknockshire about 1577, and from 1581 – 1604 he was both recorder of Brecon and attorney general for South Wales in the great sessions.

He represented the Brecon boroughs in four parliaments from 1584 – 1598. In 1589, the Earl of Pembroke put forward Williams's name to be a lawyer member of the council of the marches, but he was never in fact added to the council. In 1594 he was made a sergeant at law, and his principal real patron was thought to have been Lord Burleigh He was active as council in Westminster Hall and was soon under consideration for the bench. He was knighted on 23rd July 1603 and soon after, was appointed a 5th or additional puisne justice of the King's Bench. In 1610 he was removed from the Oxford circuit for secretly opposing the council in the marches, and for allowing recusants to swear a modified oath of allegiance. At a later Cambridge assize, he ruled that 'it was not meet to keep poor prisoners in the gaol for small matters or felonies from one assize to another' and instructed the magistrates to try petty larceny and small felonies at the quarter sessions.

Sir David died of a fever on 2nd January 1613 at Kingston House, Berks. His entrails were buried there, but then, in accordance with his will, his body was removed to St John's Chapel, now the cathedral, Brecon, which was part of the priory he owned. His extensive Welsh estates had come partly from his mother-in-laws' and his wifes', Margaret's family. She was one of the daughters of John Games of Aberbran.

Sir David Williams died a man of great living and personal wealth and his estates were inherited by his elder son, Sir Henry Williams MP.

THE WYNTER FAMILY

Wilfred de Winton

There is a memorial to this family on the floor at the entrance to the south transept. Sir William Wynter, Queen Elizabeth's admiral, is said to have been descended from an old family from Lydney in the Forest of Dean. Another member of this family was Sir John Wynter, secretary to Queen Henrietta Maria. A more distant Catholic branch lived at Huddington and produced the brothers Thomas and Robert Wynter, who were prime movers in the Gunpowder Plot.

In the list of Brecon men exhibited in the cathedral who fought at the Battle of Agincourt, there is also a Wynter, one of the few to have the distinct surname. Although the historian Theophilus Jones did not live in Brecon before the reign of Henry VIII, the name of Benedict Wynter appears in his historical writings as a burgess in the town during the lordship of the Duke of Buckingham in 1448. It is stated in Jones's history that this family formerly possessed a considerable amount of property in the parishes of Cantref, Aberysgir, Llanfihangel tal y Llyn and elsewhere.

In 1553, Andrew Wynter was High Sheriff of Brecknockshire. He had a son, Walter, who married Margaret Walwyn, daughter of the King's receiver in Brecon, and who brought to him the estate of Llanfihangel tal y Llyn. He was a Catholic, and it was his descendant, Richard Wynter, whose family rented Llangoed Castle from the Williams family during the 17th century.

The Wynters of Llanfihangel tal y Llyn conformed between 1678 and 1688; their son Edward Wynter owned Tredwstan. There are monuments to the family at Llyswen Church and Talgarth. Lewis Wynter, the physician brother of Andrew, was the ancestor of the Wynters of Brecon.

CAPTAIN FREDERICK JONES

Frederick Jones was the youngest but one of the nine children of Hannah, who inherited the Pengerrig estate in Radnorshire, close to Builth Wells, and of Thomas Jones of Cefnllys. His memorial is up on the west side of the south transept. His brother was Thomas Jones, one of the great Welsh artists. He received his teenage education, unlike his brother who was at Christ College Brecon, at Kingswood School, Bristol, which had been founded in 1748 by Charles Wesley, as his father had strong dissenting beliefs.

After school, he was accepted as a student at St Edmund Hall, Oxford. In February, 1777, he was received into the military service of the East India Company sponsored by Walter Wilkins, and on 7th March he was appointed as a cadet, assigned to the Bombay presidency of the company.

After leaving Wales, he kept a diary for almost the rest of his life. When he reached Bombay, he was informed that he'd been appointed as Lt. Fireworker in the Regiment of Artillery. The seven islands of Bombay had been given by the Portuguese to Britain as the dowry of Catherine de Braganza when she married Charles II in 1662. Frederick was involved in various military expeditions, including one against the Maharashtras in the west of India. However, the East India Company army had to retreat, and territory that had been conquered on the Island of Salsette, in the Arabian sea, had to be returned to the Maharashtras.

Frederick Jones was involved in several other campaigns, including one against Tipu Sultan of Mysore.

In 1786, Frederick was promoted to captain and was allowed to return home. Although soldiers did not benefit as much as administrators did, Frederick Jones did not return from India empty handed. On June 12th, 1795, he married Miss Anne Evans. His devotion to the family is illustrated when, at considerable expense, at least £3,000 in today's value, he erected at Caebach Chapel in 1811, a significant memorial to the Jones family of Pengerrig. Frederick Jones was very much part of the social scene in Brecon, but it must be remembered, that because of family matters, he often spent months at Pengerrig in Radnorshire. When he established himself in Brecon, he knew nobody in the town apart from his other brother Middleton, who was a solicitor, but he was well acquainted with Walter Wilkins, who lived in Glasbury. He was invited to become a member of Brecon Agricultural Show, which he accepted.

Although he lived in a large house in the Struet, he travelled a lot, sometimes on journeys lasting between six and nine weeks. He attended the theatre, bought some of his clothes from one of the most expensive tailors in London, where he also sought medical advice from one of the most eminent doctors, and occasionally had groceries and wine delivered from Bristol. He lent a number of people money, and it will never be known exactly where he obtained much of his wealth, apart from the fact that he did receive a small pension from the East

India Company. In September, 1791, he received his India savings, totalling £2,888, about £310,000 in today's money. When he died, he left the equivalent of around £400,000 to an unknown number of farms in the area.

Much of the information on Frederick Jones was taken from Ken Jones' lecture on the subject to the Brecknock Society.

THE MARQUIS OF CAMDEN

Charles Pratt

The family name was Pratt. Their origins were in Devonshire, and although their original estate had been lost because of the civil war, two generations later, the fortunes of the family appear to have been greatly restored when Sir John Pratt became Lord Chief Justice.

With the death of Sir John in 1724, his son John from his first marriage succeeded to the estates of Wildernesse Park in Kent, and in 1740, Baynham Abbey in Sussex. He was the first member of the Pratt family to make a substantial incursion into Breconshire, when, in 1718, he married Elizabeth, daughter of Sir Jeffrey Jeffreys, who had purchased the Priory estates in 1689. The second and more lasting incursion into Breconshire was that of Charles Pratt, later to be the first Earl Camden and Lord President of the council. In 1749, he married Elizabeth Jeffreys, co-heir to the substantial Priory Estates. Charles did not become a resident of Brecon, although the Camdens remained regular visitors to their estates, but they let out the Priory to Breconshire county families. From 1793, Mr Jeffrey Wilkins was tenant, and later, Thomas Wood, who was, coincidentally, the Earl of Camden's son in law. Later, William de Winton rented the building in the 1850s.

Sir Jeffrey Jeffreys was the third son of Watkin Jeffreys of Bailey Llwyel. He was educated and adopted by his uncle, Alderman John Jeffreys of London, who had made a fortune as a merchant in the metropolis. Sir Jeffrey, one of his nephews, was also a merchant of great fortune, rank and quality in London, and alderman of the city. Edward, the elder son of Sir Jeffrey, was one of the first subscribing members of Brecknock Agricultural Society.

In the memorial in the Priory Church, one of the tablets in the south transept says it is 'sacred to the memory of the Rt. Hon. John Jeffreys Pratt, Marquis of Camden KG'. He died on October 8th, 1840 aged 81 years. During a long life, passed in the service of the public and in the highest offices of state, he contributed by voluntary donations towards the exigencies of his country.

Three marquises cover the period 1840-1893; none of these gentlemen married into Breconshire society, and contented themselves with English matches. The 3rd Marquis was briefly MP for Brecon borough, but had to give up the seat on elevation to the Lords following the death of his father. During a visit to Brecon by the marquis in 1869, permission was given to build the first houses in Camden

Road. Between 1912 and 1923, the then Marquis of Camden sold a high percentage of his Welsh estates.

The next decade witnessed the virtual end of Camden influence in Wales, principally through sales. The Welsh estates of the Camden family terminated in 1946 which ended 200 years of the involvement of the Pratt family in Breconshire. Little remains to remind us of their presence. On the east side of Brecon, however, stand Camden Road and Camden Crescent and the Camden Arms public house was long registered in the Watton. A portrait of the 1st Marquis hangs in splendour in Brecon Museum.

This information is taken partly from Tony Bell's article on the Camdens in Brycheiniog.

THE VAUGHAN – MORGANS OF GLASBURY

The plaque to this family stands on the east wall of the south transept. It seems likely they were farmers originally, and only at a comparatively late date did they concentrate on the wool stapling business that was to be the foundation of their prosperity. This seems to have reached its height during the 1830s when the three partners were established in large, comfortable houses, held an assured place in local society, spent freely and appeared financially unassailable. Their business is thought to have been the largest of its kind in South Wales. The wool from the hills of mid Wales was collected here in Brecon, sorted and graded, before being sent to the Yorkshire mills by wagon and by pack horse. However, disaster befell the business. The immediate cause of their ruin is thought to have been the failure of the country banks in Yorkshire, added to the failure of the Yorkshire mills that had bought the Morgan wool, and additional embarrassment may have been the loss of markets owing to the growing imports of Australian wool.

Thomas Morgan, the 3rd brother, left for Abergavenny, where he managed The Angel Hotel, and it is his wife, Mary Anne Morgan, who lies in the south transept of Brecon Cathedral. Thomas Vaughan Morgan (1823 – 1885) took over from his father and ran The Angel with outstanding success. However, he left the hotel under stormy circumstances, and joined his brother in London.

Like Thomas, William Vaughan Morgan went to Dr Roy's School at Fulham, and was apprenticed to retail drapers in Regent Street. It seems to have been generally recognised that William was the most able businessman in the family. He was the virtual founder of Morgan Brothers and the Morgan Crucible Company; there was a factory at Battersea, and the merchandising business of Morgan Brothers in London flourished. William had several other interests, one of which was the Middlesex Infantry Militia, but his main interest outside his business was undoubtedly the promotion of homeopathy. He sought further outlets for his energies and stood as Liberal member for the Borough of Brecon in 1874, but was defeated by a small margin.

His son, Walter Vaughan Morgan (1831 – 1916) started off in the National Provincial Bank in Brecon, and at the end of four years was promoted to Manchester. He remained there for four years and was then invited to join his brothers in the business in London. He astutely guided the business and pursued his other three main interests: his old school Christ's Hospital, his civic duties in the city, and freemasonry. In 1900, he was elected Sheriff of the City of London, and was afterwards knighted for this service. Then in 1905 came his turn as Lord Mayor. He was invited down to Brecon, where he presided at a meeting of the Freemasons' Lodge, the first Worshipful Master of which had been Theophilus Jones. Afterwards he was entertained by the Freemasons to a banquet at the Castle Hotel. The next day through streets thronged with cheering crowds, he drove to the Guildhall to be presented with the Freedom of the Borough.

This family produced a number of distinguished sons and daughters, and the first and last of Breconshire's Lord Mayors of London. The Morgan Crucible firm went on for a long time, and was a successful large limited company in its day. It was a family of enterprise and initiative, which gave its prestige to the County of Brecknock, where it had originated.

The Morgan family's memorial in Brecon Cathedral is the window depicting the Adoration of the Magi, in the Laurence Chapel, given by Sir Walter Vaughan Morgan in memory of his parents. The jewelled brass altar cross was originally a gift to the parish of Glasbury, where Sir Walter was born. The late Sir Kenyon Vaughan Morgan MP and Lady Vaughan Morgan were also magnificent donors to the cathedral.

THE REGIMENTAL CHAPEL

John Henry Williams

The South Wales Borderers lost 5,777 men in the Great War, and probably three times that figure were wounded and seriously maimed for the rest of their lives. It was therefore appropriate that, when a memorial was unveiled 'To the Glorious and Immortal Memory of those men who gave their lives in the Great War' that the Havard Chapel should be designated as the Regimental chapel of the South Wales Borderers. This chapel was originally erected in the 14th century as a chantry chapel by the Havards of Pont Willim, a local family of great influence, and descendants of the Norman knight Sir Walter Havard, as previously mentioned. The chapel was formerly the Lady Chapel of the Priory Church and was known for centuries as The Vicar's Chapel. Its restoration was carried out under the supervision of a celebrated church architect, Sir Charles Nicholson Bart.

The Rolls of Honour contained in book form describes the names of the fallen for the two World Wars, and they are in a case within the reredos. Copies are available on lecterns near the entrance to the chapel for consultation. A bronze chandelier for candles, dating from 1722 has been carefully repaired and cleaned, and hung from the centre of the roof. There is a 14th century recumbent effigy monument of the Aubrey family which was removed from Christ College chapel at the Reformation. Many inscribed memorials to officers and men rest on the benches. The 24th regiment has served this country continuously for over 300 years and in the process, twenty three soldiers have been awarded the Victoria Cross. The regiment was raised by Sir Edward Dering, a Kentish baronet, and became known as the 24th regiment of foot in 1751. The regiment was linked with Warwickshire from about 31st August, 1782 and carried the title, '24th 2nd Warwickshire regiment of foot' until 1st July, 1881. The 24th Regiment had recruited in the counties of Brecknock, Cardigan, Montgomery, Monmouth and Radnor for 6 years before the Anglo Zulu War. It was the 1964 film, 'Zulu', which suggests the title of the regiment in 1879 was the South Wales Borderers, and that Welsh men formed the major element of the defenders at Rorke's Drift. Neither was true. Only about thirty soldiers of the 120 men defending the mission station were Welsh born.

The glorious defence of Rorke's Drift was commemorated by Queen Victoria in allowing a silver Wreath of Immortelles to be carried on the 'Queen's Colour'.

Among those commemorated in the chapel is Company Sergeant Major John Henry Williams, who won a VC in October 1918 during the attack on Villiers Outreaux, in northern France, when, observing that his company was suffering heavy casualties from a machine gun, he ordered a Lewis gun to engage it and went forward, under heavy fire to the flank of the enemy post, which he rushed single handed, capturing fifteen of the enemy. He was awarded three other medals for gallantry, and the King decorated him four times, for gallantry in one day.

One of the most famous names in the regimental chapel is Napier, and a number of this family served in the 24th regiment of foot. Even to this present day, Major General Lennox Napier, who recently died, and his son, Phillip rose to the rank of brigadier. The author wondered what attracted the Napiers to the 24th, as he always believed them a Scottish rather than a Welsh family. It is only latterly in their existence that the 24th became a Welsh Regiment, and they were quite slow to adopt Welsh symbols, like St David's Day and the Regimental Goat. However, today, they have joined with the Welsh regiment and the Royal Welsh Fusiliers to make a new amalgamated regiment: the Royal Welsh. They are now based at Tidworth, as one of the frontline components of the British armoured division.

With regard to the chapel, we must mention again the Wreath of Immortelles which was awarded by Queen Victoria in 1880 to the 24th, for the immemorial defence of Rorke's Drift. The colours from the Zulu war are also in the chapel.

The S W Borderers are a relatively recent regiment, compared with the Royal Welsh Fusiliers founded by a Welshman Lord Herbert, and Henry Tudor's bodyguard the Yeoman of the Guard, and the Archers at Agincourt and Crecy. As mentioned, the Borderers did not seem keen on goats or St David's Day, but it was one of their few Welsh colonels, Major General Morgan Owen who re-established the chapel at the cathedral from its original chapel in Warwick.

It was probably advantageous to the reconciliation of Wales and the Zulu nation that the 24th lost the battle of Isandlwana which has made it much easier for the 2 sides to accept each other.

THE DE WINTON FAMILY

The Wilkins family could trace their history in Breconshire back to Norman ancestors named de Wintona, hence the substitution of the surname de Winton for Wilkins by various members of the family in the 18th and 19th centuries. They had, for generations, been connected with the law, and the profitable office of Clerk of the Crown for the Brecknock circuit of the Court of Great Sessions.

In the 18th century, some members of the family became involved in the iron industry at Brecon, Hirwaun, Machen and Tredegar. Their bank, Wilkins & Co, was established in 1778, and was the sole bank of its area. During the late 18th and much of the 19th century, it was the most important banking partnership in South Wales. In 1815 it was referred to as the Brecon Bank, and by 1826 as the Brecon Old Bank. It has been suggested that the chief promoter of the bank was Walter Wilkins, who, from 1796, until his death was Whig MP for Radnorshire.

In 1759, he went to India, where he made a considerable fortune, before settling at Maes-Llwch in 1778. Some of his Indian gains undoubtedly went into the formation of the bank, and he stood high in the confidence of the Bank of England. The Wilkins Bank was well established and many of the scions of the family became involved in Brecon Cathedral.

Wilfred Seymour de Winton, may be regarded as the lay founder of our diocese, as he restored the church, the grounds, and the monastic buildings included in the precinct. He was an austere but generous man. Throughout his life of self effacement and self sacrifice he was devoted to God, his church and his fellow men. For forty years, the creation of the new diocese of Swansea and Brecon, and the transformation of the Priory Church to Brecon Cathedral were the ideals of his life. His dedication to these ideals make him one of the great churchmen of the 20th century, and there is a plaque (1856-1929) dedicated to him in the St Lawrence chapel which he himself had paid to restore.

He was never married, but his niece remembers him as 'kindly' and 'as a giver of exciting presents'. He had an important and very large ceramic collection which he gave to the National Museum in Cardiff, where it is displayed on the 1st floor.

Also involved in the restoration of the cathedral and grounds was William Francis Parry de Winton, born on 29th November 1868, and died 2nd April 1962, who was nine times mayor of Brecon. Another de Winton involved was John Crichton Parry de Winton, 1905 – 1976, who had an MA from Oxford and was in the Royal Naval Volunteer Reserve in World War II. This remarkable family showed huge affection for Brecon Cathedral, and backed it up with their money and resources.

FIGURES ON THE REREDOS

BISHOP HUGH GORE

The elder son of John Gore, and a relative of the Earls of Arran, Hugh was born in Dorset, sent to school at Lismore in Ireland, and then proceeded to Trinity College, Oxford. His first preferment was believed to have been the living of Nicholaston, and the rectory of Oxwich. He was ejected under the Propagation Act of 1650, and subsequently kept a school for some years in Swansea.

After the Restoration, he received preferment in Ireland, becoming bishop of

Waterford and Lismore in 1666. In 1682, his affection for the town of Swansea and its people led him to endow a free grammar school for the sons of the poorer of the burgesses. Gore retired to Swansea to live in 1869, died, and was buried in St Mary's Church there on 27th March, 1691.

HENRY VAUGHAN

Henry Vaughan is a figure in the reredos in the cathedral, and he did much of his courting of his first wife, Catherine Wise there. The Priory grove is a wooded area belonging to Brecon Priory, which was the home of Sir Herbert Price. Price had close connections with the Wise family from Coleshill in Warwickshire. It is likely that Vaughan first met Catherine when she was visiting the Priory, and his poem,

'Upon the priory grove, his usual retirement' reflects betrothal or marriage and blessings are called down upon the happy couple. In the final paragraph, Vaughan looks beyond the present to the future in which the grove will be transplanted to a realm beyond decay and death, and where it will once again witness the innocent passion of the transfigured couple whose love first flourished beneath its shade.

Vaughan's pedigree was impressive, being related to Sir Roger Vaughan who commanded bands of the Welsh archers at Agincourt; also to the Herberts of Raglan, and the Somersets. Henry, in writing to one of the Aubreys in later life, says, "My brother and I were born at Newton in the parish of St Bridgets in the year 1621." Not a stone remains in its original place in the present house of Newton which is situated between Scethrog and Llansantffraed under the wooded hillside of Allt-yr-Esgair. Vaughan, in many ways, was a home bird who needed his roots. He felt inspired by the mythology and magic of Wales although his religious background was devoutly Christian and Anglican.

At a relatively early age Henry went up to Jesus College, Oxford which was full of Welshmen at that time. It had been founded by Dr Hugh Price, a Brecon butcher's son, at the behest of Elizabeth 1. Henry is not recorded as matriculating but probably used it as a sort of finishing school from whence to go on to study law in London. On arriving in London he entered the Parliamentary' lions' den'. With the outbreak of the Civil War the King moved his court to Oxford. In the May Day riots of 1640 before the outbreak of war, great crowds gathered, demonstrating against the hated Archbishop Laud.

Vaughan spent some time in the taverns sampling the atmosphere of wildness and some elegance. His twin brother, Thomas, was committed to the King's side. In 'Misery', one of his poems at the time, he talks about the age, *'The present times are not to snudge in and embrace a cot. Action and blood now get the game, I'd loose those knots thine hands did tie then would go travel, fight or die.'* His brother, William, died of war wounds in 1648. Henry Vaughan had himself gone to war against the Roundheads in 1645 and it is not surprising that Vaughan's vocabulary was often of war; there seems to be a perpetual obsession with blood, blows and glory. Henry was appalled at the Cavalier defeat. He talks about his world being subject to vast movements of violence. His elegies on Mr R W, killed at the Battle of Rowten Heath in 1645 and on Mr R Hall, killed at Pontefract in 1648, talk about the Cavalier martyr *'As some star hurled in diurnal motions from afar'*.

In Brecon, Colonel Herbert Price was the governor of Brecon Castle and MP for the town; he headed the Vaughans' regiment at Chester. In April 1644 Price raised troops for the King in Brecon and, the following summer, entertained King Charles at the Priory. It is possible that Vaughan could have met him there, for of course, this is where Vaughan did much of his courting of Catherine Wise. The King certainly made a great impression on Vaughan, who was anguished at Charles's death. There is not a lot of evidence of Vaughan's military service, although in the poem, *'Upon a cloak lent him by Mr J Ridsley',* he talks about the adventures of a rough cloak and shows himself as a soldier present at the rough siege of Chester. It is probable he was at the Battle of Rowten Heath in 1645, which marked the defeat of the Cavaliers, when the King was forced to retreat to Chester. However, after the battle itself, the remnant of the Royalist army retreated to Beeston Castle upon whose surrender in 1645 the defeated Cavaliers were allowed to march across the Dee into Denbigh in North Wales.

Meanwhile, the inhabitants of Brecon had pulled down their town walls to prevent devastation and eventually welcomed the Parliamentary troops. It was then downhill all the way for Henry Vaughan and his family. Their devotion to the King's cause made them outcasts in their own world and, although it is probable that Henry accepted the sufferings and roughness of war because of his devotion to the Royalist cause, he later became much more of a pacifist in his outlook, which was more acceptable to his mysticism and peaceful poetry in the Usk valley. The war was a huge upheaval, after his childhood in gentle, gentrified Breconshire and brought him face to face with the realities of death and ruthless politics. Civil war is never easy for any country and Henry's life was moulded by its reality and by the defeat of high Anglicanism and the descent into fundamental Puritanism. The latter went against the temperament and instinct of Henry Vaughan who, although always a Welshman, felt he had to take sides in a conflict that turned his fellow countrymen against one another.

There is not a lot of war poetry in his writing but, what there is, is concerned with heroism and the rightness of the King's cause. Neither is there much evidence of his relationship with his fellow soldiers. His mind and spirit were not destroyed by cynicism and bitterness because his poetry, with its great themes of God and wonder and the supernatural, continued to be created long after the War. One of the great metaphysical poets from Wales, like his cousin George Herbert who represented the Celtic affinity with the supernatural, Vaughan was born a Welshman, lived in Wales most of his life, and his destiny was tied up with the cruel times he lived in.

Siegfried Sassoon's poem, '*On the Grave of Henry Vaughan*' sums him up and reads as follows:

> '*Above the voiceful windings of a river*
>
> *An old green slab of simply graven stone*
>
> *Shuns notice, overshadowed by a yew.*
>
> *Here Vaughan lies dead, whose name flows on for ever*
>
> *Through pastures of the spirit washed with dew*
>
> *And starlit with eternities unknown.*
>
> *Here sleeps the Silurist; the loved physician;*
>
> *The face that left no portraiture behind;*
>
> *The skull that housed white angels and had vision*
>
> *Of daybreak through the gateways of the mind.*
>
> *Here faith and mercy, wisdom and humility*
>
> *(Whose influence shall prevail for evermore)*

Shine. And this lowly grave tells Heaven's tranquillity
And here stand I, a suppliant at the door.'
'Henry Vaughan: The Complete Poems' edited by Alan Rudrum

DR HUGH PRICE

Hugh Price

Hugh Price, 1495-1574, lawyer, clergyman and founder of Jesus College Oxford, is also on the reredos in the cathedral. He was the son of Rhys ap Rhys, a butcher in the town of Brecon, who acquired such a fortune as to enable him to give his children a liberal education, and to leave to his elder son a considerable estate. Price was educated at Oxford, where he graduated as Bachelor of Civil Law on 4th July, 1512.

On 26th April, 1532, he was one of those who tried James Bainham, an English lawyer and Protestant reformer, for heresy in the Tower of London. On the refoundation of the See of Rochester in 1541, he was appointed to be the 1st prebend and from 1571 to 1574, he was treasurer of St David's. According to the archivist of Jesus College, he was buried in the Priory Church of Brecon in August, 1574, although there is no evidence of a tomb at the cathedral.

On Price's petition, and by letters patent dated 27th June, 1571, Elizabeth I established Jesus College, Oxford as a Welsh Protestant College. Price left land worth £60 per year to the college. It was the first college to be founded at Oxford after the Reformation, and the first distinctly Protestant one. The buildings were commenced in about 1572, but only two storeys on the east and south sides of the outer quadrangle were completed by 1618. A portrait of Price, attributed to Holbein, belongs to the college.

PRELATES AND PASTORS

EDWARD WILLIAM WILLIAMSON 1892 – 1953
BISHOP OF SWANSEA & BRECON

Bishop Edward Williamson

Educated at Llandaff School and Westminster School, he was a King's scholar at Christchurch, Oxford. He was appointed warden of St Michael's College, Llandaff, in 1926 and remained there until he was elected Bishop of Swansea & Brecon in 1939. Even though he was not a Welshman, he loved Wales, its Church and its people. When he was invited early in 1953 to become one of the vice presidents of the Eisteddfod in Ystradgynlais in 1954, his letter of acceptance was written in Welsh. He died suddenly, during the meeting of the governing body of the Church in Wales at Llandrindod, and, only a few minutes before, he had made a powerful speech deploring the exodus of young Welsh priests to England. He was at his best among the students at St Michael's College where his quiet charm and sound learning influenced generations of ordinands.

No other prelates have an obvious mention in the cathedral, but the author would like to remember Bishop Jack Thomas, who was a great friend of his father and a beautifully spiritual man, also Bishop Glyn Simon, who became Archbishop of Wales and was an intellectual and academic leader of the Church in Wales, on which he had a tremendous influence. Bishop John Davies, who had been Dean of the cathedral and then was the first Bishop of Swansea & Brecon to become Archbishop of Wales, has also to be mentioned. His inspiration of instituting a choir trust fund has done so much to help the music in the cathedral, and he is a man who has the common touch and is able to communicate with all sorts and different kinds of people. Another bishop the author did not know well, although he sent a painted coconut to him from Belize, formerly British Honduras, was Bishop Benjamin Vaughan, who had been bishop in that central American country. These bishops simply give us a flavour of the priests involved with the cathedral, and in no way are they supposed to be a full account of all the priests who officiated there.

EDWARD LATHAM BEVAN

Edward Latham Bevan was the first Bishop of Swansea and Brecon. He is immortalised in the Goscombe John bronze at the entrance to the St Lawrence Chapel. He was a man of simple faith, making no pretensions to scholarship, who had an abundance of the quality of entering into the thought and feelings of everyone he met with empathy, a quality we associate with that saint the old bishop resembled in so many ways, St Barnabus the Apostle, about whom it was written by St Luke that 'He was a good man, and full of the Holy Ghost'. Aristocratic in bearing and voice, Bevan never conveyed a feeling of superiority or pomposity, even when expressing a note of objection or displeasure.

Bishop Bevan

53

BISHOP WILLIAM THOMAS HAVARD 1889 – 1956

Bishop William Thomas Havard

The Havard Chapel probably has its roots in the Havard family, descended from Sir Walter Havard, one of the original Norman knights in Brecknockshire and it is probably not coincidental that Bishop Havard has the same name. He was educated at the University College of Wales, Aberystwyth and Jesus College, Oxford. Between 1915 and 1919, he was chaplain to the armed forces, and he was mentioned in Dispatches in 1916 and awarded the Military Cross in 1917, although the author cannot find any details of these actions. He did wonderful work acting as chaplain to the 1st Volunteer battalion the South Wales Borderers in the Great War and was a huge help to young soldiers on a vigorous and exhausting march to Lahej in Yemen. The return march to Aden was of even greater stress.

He gained fame as a rugby player at Aberystwyth, won his cap for Wales against New Zealand in 1919 and gained his rugby blue whilst at Oxford. He married in 1922, Florence Aimee Holmes, and they had two sons and two daughters. He was a powerful preacher in both Welsh and English, and often preached at the services broadcast on the Sundays previous to the National Eisteddfodau. He became chaplain of Jesus College, Oxford, and was consecrated Bishop of St Asaph in September, 1934. After sixteen years, he was translated to St David's in 1950.

He died on 17th August, 1956 and was buried at Brecon.

It is interesting to note that the present leader of Powys County Council, Rosemary Harris, is directly descended from the Havards.

THE SCULPTORS

SIR WILLIAM GOSCOMBE JOHN 1860 – 1952

Sir William Goscombe John

As a young man, he assumed the name Goscombe from a Gloucestershire village near his mother's old home. His father was a wood carver in the workshop set up by Lord Bute for the restoration of Cardiff Castle. He was trained in Cardiff, and later in London at the City & Guilds Kensington School of Art and from1884 at the Royal Academy Schools. In 1889, he won the RA's gold medal.

John's numerous public statues included those of the 7th Duke of Devonshire at Eastbourne, and equestrian statues of Edward VIII at Cape Town, and also of Lord Tredegar. He returned to London in 1891 and settled in 1892 in St John's Wood. He had spent some time in Paris beforehand, where he watched Rodin work, and thus showed a complete anatomical mastery and suave rhythm in his nudes. In 1916, he contributed a marble figure of St David, one of a group of ten figures commissioned by Lord Rhondda for Cardiff City Hall. He designed the regalia used for the Investiture of the Prince of Wales at Caernarvon in 1911, and in the same year he was knighted at Bangor.

John was an academic sculptor first and last; having first shown at the RA in 1896, he continued to exhibit there annually until 1968, a period of sixty two years. He was a courteous man, proud of his Welsh nationality, but somewhat reserved. He married Anna Marthe Weiss, daughter of Paul Wiess, the engraver. Their only child, Muriel Goscombe married Frederick Luke Val Fildes, the son of the painter Sir Luke Fildes. He died on 15th December, 1952 in St John's Wood, and was buried in Hampstead Cemetery in the tomb which he had sculpted for his wife.

John's style underwent little change throughout his long life, apart from a broadening of the treatment of busts and war memorials. Most of these were in bronze or marble, and in both of these he was a convincing and accurate portrayer of character. His bronze of Edward Latham Bevan lies near the south transept in Brecon Cathedral, and he is said to have designed the Bishop's Throne in the Cathedral.

JOHN EVAN THOMAS

Born in Brecon on15th January, 1810, he studied in London under Chantrey, the leading portrait sculptor in the Regency era, and afterwards on the continent. He began to work independently in 1834, and was a frequent exhibitor at the Royal Academy between 1835 and 1857. Two of his principal works are considered to be

'The 2nd Marquis of Londonderry' at Westminster Abbey and

'The 2nd Marquis of Bute' in Cardiff City Centre. Four more principal works are 'Sir Charles Morgan' at Newport, 'The Duke of Wellington' at Brecon, and 'John Henry Vivian' at Swansea. In Brecknock Museum, a metal electrotype of his 1814 plaster sculpture 'Death of Tewdrig' depicts the dying 5th century King Tewdrig, Saint of Glamorgan. He retained the patronage of the Welsh landed gentry, producing bust portraits of them and there is a lot of his statue work in the northern transept of Brecon Cathedral. For thirty years, he was assisted in his work by his brother William Meredith Thomas, who helped complete many of his elder brother's unfinished works. He was a Welshman through and through and took a great interest in anything pertaining to Wales. He played a leading part, with the support of Lord Llanover, in the movement to prevent any misuse of the endowments of Christ College Brecon. He bought Penisha'r-Pentre, a little mansion at Llanspyddid. and 1868, he became Sheriff of Brecknock. John Evan Thomas died on 9th October 1873 in London and was buried there.

THE ROOD CROSS

Brecon's Rood Cross returned after nearly 500 years.

The Rood Cross

In 1538 King Henry VIII destroyed Brecon's rood screen, the division between the monks and the people in the Priory Church, now the Cathedral. On the screen had hung a gold crucifix which people from all over Wales and beyond had come on pilgrimage to touch as they prayed for healing.

Now a life size bronze crucifix has been hung near where the rood screen used to be. This new artwork has been very generously given to the Cathedral; the necessary Faculties having been obtained.

Anthony Bunker, a Welsh-born lawyer, friend of Artes Mundi and on the board of Welsh National Opera, commissioned this crucifix to celebrate his wife Elizabeth's ordination to the priesthood.

The artist is Helen Sinclair, born in 1954 in South Wales. Since studying at the Wimbledon School of Art and teaching for twelve years, Helen has been a full-time sculptor since 1988. She exhibits widely throughout England and Wales and has work in private collections all over the world.

The crucifix weighs 90 kg and was cast from driftwood Helen picked up on Rhossili beach, near her home on the Gower Peninsula. It was hung by Damon Bramley from the trap door in the tower which is otherwise used to lower the bells to ground level on the rare occasions when they need repairing or replacing.

THE ARTISTS OF THE ORIGINAL PAINTINGS

'The Baptism of Christ' stands on the altar in the Havard Chapel, and is attributed to Francesco Albani, who was born in Bologna in Italy, in 1578. By the age of twelve, he had become apprenticed to the competent Mannerist painter, Dennis Calvert, the Flemish born painter in whose studio he met Guido Reni. He soon followed Reni to the so-called academy run by Annibale in Bologna. Albani became one of Annibale's most successful apprenticeships. Albani's best frescos are those on mythological subjects and among the best known of his sacred subjects are 'St Sebastian' and 'An Assumption of The Virgin'. The painting in Brecon Cathedral is thought to be of his school but may not have been painted by Albani himself.

Gerard von Honthorst

Gerard von Honthorst, whose painting hangs to the left of the altar, was a Dutch Golden Age painter, who became especially noted for his depiction of artificially lit scenes. Early in his career he visited Rome, where he had great success painting in a style influenced by Caravaggio. He returned to Utrecht in1620, and went on to build a considerable reputation both in the Dutch Republic and abroad. In 1623, the year of his marriage, he was president of the Guild of St Luke in Utrecht. He soon became so fashionable that Sir Dudley Carlton, then English envoy at the Hague, recommended his works to the Earl of Arundel and Lord Dorchester. After his return to Utrecht, Honthorst retained the patronage of the English monarch, painting for him in 1631 a large picture of the King and Queen of Bohemia. His popularity in the Netherlands was such that he opened a second studio in the Hague where he painted portraits of members of the court, and taught drawing. These large studios, where the work included making replicas of Honthorst's royal portraits employed a large number of students and assistants.

Another painting of significance in the cathedral is 'Peace', by the artist William Strutt. It was presented to the cathedral in memory of Cecil Frederick Gilbertson, honorary secretary of the diocesan board of finance, 1924-47, by his wife and children. The artist, whose dates are 1825-1915 is not well known in Britain today, but he enjoys a considerable reputation in Australia, where his large history paintings hang in major galleries. He was the son of a Bank of England clerk, and his grandfather was the artist and engraver Joseph Strutt, who produced some fine colour illustrations in a volume of colour plate books. William received the greatest part of his artistic education in France, which included instruction at the Ecole de Beaux Arts, by Paul de la Roche. He was apprenticed in 1843-4 to Jouy, a pupil of Angres, a French NeoClassical painter, and for the next three years he prepared drawings for illustrated books. By 1850, however, seized with the urge to seek new fields, he sailed for Melbourne, Australia, then a boom town at the height of the Gold Rush. He made water colours and drawings of the diggings at Ballarat. In 1855, he purchased land in Taranaki in New Zealand, where he settled briefly with his wife and family, eventually returning to Melbourne and from there back to England.

These paintings in the Cathedral are for the most part authentic, although, as mentioned, the Albani one may be of his school.

The Pulpit Crucifix

Two carvings, '*The Last Supper*' and '*The Pulpit Crucifix*' were donated to Brecon Cathedral in 1993 by Canon AG Lewis (1915-2008), former vicar of Aberyscir, Ystalyfera and Coelbren. 'Griff,' as he was known to his many friends, was educated at St David's College Lampeter. He served with the South Wales Borderers and spent his whole career as a clergyman in the Diocese of Swansea and Brecon. Griff retired to Brecon with his wife Sylvia in 1989 and both continued to support the Cathedral as welcomers and regular communicants for many years. Sylvia Lewis (nee Jayne) grew up in Lampeter where her great uncle Francis Jayne was formerly the principal of St David's College (1879-1886). A graduate of Wadham College Oxford, he was also Fellow of Jesus College Oxford and became Bishop of Chester in 1889, a post he held until 1919.

Both carvings were a gift to the Lewis family from Adelina Patti the world famous 19th century Italian opera singer, former of Craig Y Nos castle in the Swansea Valley. The inscriptions on both carvings are in German which suggests that Germany is the country of origin, possibly dating back to the latter part of the 19th century. The name Oberammergau, famous for its tradition in woodcarvings and the world famous Passion Play is engraved on the *Last Supper* carving, suggesting that the town is the origin of the works. The Lewis family lived for nearly a hundred years in Callwen Vicarage where Rhys was born in 1915. His uncle, the Reverend David Jenkin Hughes was vicar of Callwen Church, and chaplain to Adelina Patti.

The Last Supper

JOSEPH RICHARD COBB

There is a memorial at the top of the nave to Joseph Cobb, landowner, businessman and antiquarian, who played a prominent role in the life of Brecon in the second half of the 19th century. He was a ruthless businessman, who acquired huge wealth, and in today's terms, he would be described as a multi-millionaire. He was very instrumental in Gilbert Scott's restoration of Brecon Cathedral, to such an extent that the erection of the lychgate was dedicated to him. The family lived in Monmouthshire, and there is some perception that he was a pupil at Christ College, although there is no record of it. He was a governor there from 1871 until the year he died in 1897. A portrait of him still hangs in the school dining hall, and his benefaction to the school was the Parry de Winton scholarship, named after his father-in-law, of £40 a year, to boys leaving the school for Oxford or Cambridge.

With his father-in-law, John Parry de Winton, Cobb was a huge enthusiast for bringing the railway line to Brecon, and he served as secretary to the company which did this for more than a quarter of a century. He particularly enabled the completion of the line from Talyllyn to Brecon in 1864 and designed the building of six terraced cottages nearby to house railway workers. The cottages, known as Cobb's Town, remain there to this day.

By the 1870s, Cobb had acquired enough money from his holdings in property and land to go for a riskier enterprise. He was brought in as a partner by Mordecai Jones, a colliery owner, who had bought the mineral rights to the land around Mardy Farm at the top of the Rhondda Fach. Cobb brought in the capital to sink the no. 1 pit, which was fortunate in hitting a rich seam of coal. The Cobb family were still receiving a share of ground rents and farm rents from the Mardy estate until the nationalisation of the coal industry in 1947.

The monument in Brecon Cathedral styles him as 'Lord of the Manor of Brecon and Caldicot'. These were titles acquired by him rather than awarded to him. The will of Joseph Cobb, written in August 1894, shows more about the extent of the land and property he owned. He bequeathed all his real estate in the counties of

Brecon, Monmouth, Warwick and Pembroke to his wife Emily, which included the family house, Nythfa, in Brecon, and Caldicot Castle. Other properties were in Swansea, Pembroke, Shropshire and Essex, and these he divided amongst his children. The complicated division of his considerable wealth created disputes ending at one stage in the High Court of Chancery. Nythfa remained the family home until 1964. His granddaughter Muriel lived there from 1926 with her husband Hugh Fowler. Nythfa was sold in 1964 for the relatively low price of £11,500 and the whole family was devastated at the loss of the family home.

This information is partly taken from Glyn Mathias's article on the Cobbs in Brycheiniog.

THE ORGANISTS

David Gedge

David Gedge gave more than 40 years service as organist and choirmaster of Brecon Cathedral. He and his wife Hazel, also an excellent organist, were a husband and wife team in the fullest sense. In 2006, they were each awarded the Cross of St Augustine; the citation for the award, signed by The Archbishop of Canterbury, Dr Rowan Williams, records that over the past four decades, Hazel had been the partner that David needed, loving, caring, understanding, unselfish and forgiving. David devoted the whole of his professional life to the worship of

God through sacred music. He appreciated the whole spectrum of beauty offered by the cathedral, which went beyond his beloved music to include the colour and form of art and architecture to be found in the cathedral. He helped innumerable young people from the least privileged areas of Brecon find purpose, comradeship and fulfilment as cathedral choristers. His support for them extended beyond the choir room to social and educational help in hundreds of different ways. He was aggrieved, sometimes, at his treatment by some of the clergy, who didn't seem to recognise his intrinsic saintliness.

David and Hazel worked for a pittance, although also, to survive financially, David became head of music at Builth Wells High School.

The present Archbishop of Wales, John Davies, when Dean of Brecon, wrote to David after his first Holy Week in Brecon, to thank him for having shared, 'In an enriching journey of faith'; he continued, 'What I believe and actually experienced was Anglicanism at its best, worship composed of a rich mixture of teaching, ceremonial, music, prayer and scripture.' The author does not have the information available to talk about other organists, but he is glad to recognise the Gedges and their enormous contribution to the cathedral.

As an adjunct to the Gedges, he would like to remember Kelvin Redford, a great schoolmaster at Christ College, Brecon, who did so much to help the Gedges. It was a wonderful era at Brecon Cathedral, and although David had a number of fallouts, so many look back at his time there with such fondness, not forgetting the work he put in to the Cathedral Choir and Singers and their successful concerts and tours.

THE VAUGHAN WATKINS

There are a number of memorials to this family on the walls of the north transept, created by Evan Thomas. Colonel Vaughan Watkins was first elected mayor of Brecon in January, 1836. He was for many years a prominent member of the Common Council, a Worshipful Master of the Old Loyal Cambrian Lodge of Freemasons at Brecon, a member of the first Board of Health, Justice of the Peace, High Sheriff in 1836, and Lord Lieutenant 1847 – 1865. He was also MP for the borough.

He rebuilt Penoyre, which was said to have cost him £100,000, a huge sum of money in those days. However, heavy taxes, the outlay on building the mansion together with its upkeep all proved a grave strain on the Colonel's resources. He was a man of great generosity to personal friends and to the locality in general. But the time came when he could no longer afford to live in the mansion he had built, and he was compelled to move from this palatial residence into the Old Bear Hotel in Ship Street, Brecon. The last days of the colonel were spent in comparative poverty; nevertheless, he retained to the end the respect and affection of the people of Brecon. And when he died, a great gathering attended his funeral which was accompanied by much civil and military ceremonial seldom seen in the district before. He was interred in the family vault in Llandefaelog. He was a great man, who fell on hard times.

SIR JOHN MEREDITH

Also in the north transept, above the door is a memorial to Sir John Meredith, a native of Radnorshire, who was born in 1714. He was High Sheriff of Brecknock in 1762, the year of his knighthood, and also of Radnorshire in 1780. He was Howell Harris's man of law and many letters passed between them which are preserved in the Trefecca Collection in the National Library of Wales. He died on 6th March, 1780.

SIR JOHN PRYSE OF BRECON

As far as I can see, there is no memorial to Sir John Pryse, but there is a brass epitaph to his second son Richard Pryse, on the back of the reredos. John Pryse was one of Brecon's most accomplished sons. He was born in 1502 on the threshold of a huge new century in British history and would become a greatly valued and amply rewarded servant of three successive Tudor monarchs. One of the earliest of Welsh Renaissance scholars, he was the first man to publish a printed book in the Welsh language.

He was born in Brecon, a flourishing market town, and was reputed to be a descendant of such a notable ancestor as Dafydd Gam. He could well have been educated at the Friary, and possibly in a Bardic school. Pryse was a bright boy and learned enough to be fit for entry to Oxford University. At the university he would have studied the arts first of all and later proceeded to study civil law, graduating as a Bachelor of Civil Law on 24th February, 1524. Then he was admitted to the Middle Temple in London in November of the same year. Middle Temple was interesting, since it had a reputation of being more selective in its choice of students than the other inns of court. When Pryse left the inn at Middle Temple, he embarked on what was to become a glittering career. As a result of his service for the Earl of Arundel, one of the great lords of the Welsh Marches, he was commended to the notice of the great Thomas Cromwell, and from there entered the employment of King Henry VIII.

In 1534-35, he began to figure largely in the legal examination of front ranking servants of the king, such as Bishop John Fisher and the former Lord Chancellor, Sir Thomas More. His links with Thomas Cromwell were increased when Pryse entered into marriage with Johane Williamson, who was a niece of Cromwell's wife Elizabeth. The year 1535 saw the King and Cromwell taking the first steps to dissolving the monasteries and Pryse was chosen as one of the three most influential visitors of the religious houses. Pryse, all the time he was involved in these investigations, was looking out for the treasures to be found in the monastic libraries. He managed to trim his sails enough to be able to successfully weather the storm of Cromwell's fall and he was still in favour with Henry. It was in the year 1540 that he took a lease of St Guthlac's Benedictine Priory and moved to live in Hereford, where he made his home for the rest of his life.

Pryse was to be appointed to the important office of Secretary to the Council of the Marches, a position that he would hold until his death in 1555. He became attached to William Herbert, later Earl of Pembroke, and President of the Council of the Marches 1550 – 1553, and before that, to Roland Lee, also a former President of the Council. He was said to be a crucial advisor to Henry VIII and Thomas Cromwell on the subject of the union of the two countries, England and Wales. In 1537 he was Commissioner for receiving dissolved monastic lands in Breconshire, including those of Brecon Priory. Early in 1547 he was recognised with the award of a knighthood.

In his native County of Breconshire, he was appointed Sheriff in 1542-3, and made a Justice of the Peace in 1543; he was also elected Bailiff of Brecon for 1544-5. He served as Member of Parliament for Breconshire in 1547 and sat in three other constituencies for parliament at different times. It is thought that the radical changes of Edward VI's reign with regard to Protestantism had left him, like many others, feeling deeply uneasy, and it was rather paradoxical that he was seen to support Queen Mary. He was one of the earliest, distinctively Welsh, Renaissance humanists, devoted to books and scholarship for most of his life, and was one of the great collectors of monastic manuscripts.

Pryse became lessee of Brecon Priory in 1537 and bought it and its estates outright in 1542. He was a huge enthusiast of books to be published in the Welsh language and was very much a Welsh patriot. His major work was the 'Historiae Britannicae Defensio', ('The Defence of British History'), a substantial tome of 160 pages, which Pryse wrote in Latin. His will is the sort of document one might expect from a learned, experienced and deeply patriotic lawyer. He provided generously for his widow and his ten surviving children, five sons and five daughters, and for close friends and servants. Pryse left a bequest of £20, a large sum in those days for the poor householders of Brecon, and £10 for mending Brecon Bridge. One of the greatest bards of 16th century Wales was Lewis Morgannwg, who hailed Pryse's Welsh *Marchog Brycheiniog a'i chefn, Dawn wendref Hondi windref ,*'which translates, *'Brecknock knight and her backbone inspiration of Honddu's fair borough and her fount of wine.'*

THE CHURCHYARD

In the churchyard of Brecon Cathedral, there is a grave with a handsome headstone which reads:

'Ci git Francois Husson

Prisonnier de guerre,

Francois Capne an 4me Regt

D'artillerie de Marine

Decede le 27 Avril 1810

age de 48 ans'.

'By foreign hands his humble grave adorned.

By strangers honour'd and by strangers mourn'd.'

There was a Captain Francois Husson of the 4th Artillery Regiment of Marines who was a prisoner of war. It is somewhat of a mystery why he joined the marines when he enlisted on 10th June 1781. He was part of a detachment of marines on board the French frigate 'Le President', which was captured by HMS Canapus and HMS Despatch. He was paroled and Brecon was one of the towns offered to him.

He and his fellow officers came to Brecon in October 1806, joining twenty one other prisoners already there. Between 1806 and 1812, there was a total number of eighty six French officers paroled in Brecon, where they would have liberty to walk on the great turnpike road, within the distance of one mile of the extremities of the town, but must not go into any field or crossroads, nor be absent from their lodgings after five o'clock in the afternoon during six winter months from October to March, nor after eight o'clock during the summer months. The government of the day gave them a meagre allowance, but they very much relied on the charity of the local community. Little is known of Francois Husson, but it is possible that he may have been befriended by the Williams family of Penpont. Many of the prisoners used their skills to make things or build stone walls, and many of those in the Senni Valley are said to have been built by the prisoners.

There is a reference to a French army officer from the Napoleonic Wars who died at Penpont while on parole. Captain Husson is the only French officer lying in the Cathedral graveyard; apparently he left no pension, he was unmarried, and the reason for his death at the age of forty eight is obscure.

Napoleonic Wars

Another famous grave is that of Captain Charles Lumley. Captain Charles Lumley VC was born in Foress House, Morayshire, about 1824. He was commissioned as an ensign into the 97th Regiment of Foot on 30th August, 1834. He became a captain and was awarded the Victoria Cross for action during the Redan, Sebastapol on 8th September 1855. He was one of the first inside the earthwork, where he was immediately engaged with three Russian gunners who were reloading a field piece and attacked him. He shot two of them with his revolver, when he was knocked down by a stone which stunned him for a moment, but on recovery he drew his sword and was in the act of cheering the men on when he received a ball in the mouth which wounded him most severely. He was decorated with the VC by H M Queen Victoria at the first VC Investiture held at Hyde Park, London on June 26th 1857. In 1857-8, he was transferred to the 2nd 23rd Regiment of Foot. He became commanding officer of that regiment's detachment at Brecon on 20th July 1858.

However, sadly, he shot himself in the head at Brecon on 17th October, 1858 and died within a few hours. An inquest which met a few days later gave a verdict of suicide due to temporary insanity. Apparently, he had recently, before his death, been absent in manner and hot tempered. He had lately been considerably worried by overwork, having to act as paymaster to the detachment and he frequently complained of not being able to properly attend his duties as commanding officer. When his remains were interred with full military honours, the whole of the garrison and militia joined the procession, during which, as it wound its slow progress through the streets, the excellent band of the militia played the mournful Sicilian Mariners' Hymn which was a very imposing spectacle.

THE COPPOCK GATES

The Coppock Gates

The Coppock Gates are situated in the Cathedral Close and are named after a famous Brecon doctor, Dr Robin Copppock. His involvement in the Cathedral was a pretty close one, and arose out of his religious beliefs. He was a sidesman and the diocesan doctor. In the war he was in the Royal Naval Commandos in a specialist unit created to organise beach landings after some spectacular failings. It was operational only from 1942-45. They all went through the Commando training course and were entitled to wear the Green Beret. Their motto was 'First in, last out' as they were the first onto the beaches and the last off. He was a beachmaster in the Sicilian landings and his commanding officer recommended him for a DSC because of his outstanding performance. He said, 'Coppock, my sub-lieutenant who joined the party as a midshipman, was a really magnificent example to everyone. He was hit by shell fragments when he first landed, but despite this, kept going throughout the entire operation without exception. Whatever happened on that beach left him completely unperturbed and I was very proud to have him in my party. I recommended him for the Distinguished Service Cross.'

We all know what an outstanding doctor he was. His service to his patients in Brecon was inestimable. Nothing was ever too much trouble despite in those days there being many late nights and long-distance visits. The depth of his care and his insight was remarkable. He knew everyone and he knew how the Brecon families all linked together. His interest had no boundaries or limits. Everyone mattered.

Robin Coppock was a much loved doctor in Brecon for many years, and his wife Dr Mary Coppock was a great support, a doctor in her own right, who was a proficient musician and a great lover of the arts and travel. He was a great friend of the author's father the Rev. Rex Morgan and cared for him until his death at the age of seventy. It is so fitting that these gates are named in his memory.

THE PARAVICINI GATES

Nicolas Paravicini was the grandson of the Swiss Ambassador to the Court of St. James, Charles Paravicini. One of the sons from his first marriage was Derek Paravicini, born 1979, a blind, autistic savant and musical prodigy. In 1986, having divorced his first wife, Nicolas married Susan Rose (Suki) Phipps who was the daughter of Alan Phipps who died in the Battle of the Island of Leros, Dodecanese, Greece, in 1943.

Suki's mother was the Hon. Nell Fraser, daughter of Lord Lovat and was brought up by Fitzroy Maclean, one of the inspirations for James Bond.

Latterly, the Paravicinis lived in Glyn Celyn, a rather splendid country house outside Brecon. They have done much philanthropic work for Brecon Cathedral and have been tireless workers on its behalf; thus, in gratitude, the gates below the Diocesan Centre have been named after them.

THE RESTORING ARCHITECTS

Gilbert Scott

GILBERT SCOTT

Gilbert Scott (1811-1878) was one of the foremost restoring architects of his day. He began his career modestly enough as a pupil of James Edmeston Snr. and a designer of workhouses. In 1840 he won the competition to design the Protestant Martyrs' memorial in Oxford. Scott was appointed restoring architect to Ely Cathedral in 1847 and from then on his advice was sought for all sorts of schemes involving the restoration of many medieval buildings. He visited Brecon and the cathedral on many occasions from 1847 onwards, sketching details and making notes of what needed doing. His main recommendations were to check the foundations of the outer walls and repair as necessary, repair the roof and upper storeys of the tower, clean all the limewash off the stone dressings but preserve all ancient colouring, restore the transept roofs to their original pitch, take up and relay all the floors, remove Wyatt's screen and complete the chancel vaulting. In comparison with other contemporary restorations, it was fairly conservative. The chancel roof was raised from its 15th century low pitch to the original steep pitch.

W.D.CAROE

William Douglas Caroe (1858-1938) was trained in the office of JL Pearson, designer of Truro Cathedral. He was architect to the ecclesiastical commissioners of 1895 undertaking a considerable number of restorations in Wales. In Brecon Cathedral he completed the reconstruction of the south east chapels as the Chapel of St Lawrence and a sacristy. He also built the reredos and a new organ chamber above the ante chapel. The final addition to the cathedral was severely practical with the flat roof fuel store and boiler room tucked out of sight in the south of the west end. Various other alterations to the choir pews also took place, together with the moving of the pulpit.

These two architects both had an impact but did not severely alter the medieval construction of Brecon Cathedral. Their involvement, however, put it on a sounder footing.

CONCLUSION

In conclusion, Brecon Cathedral has a huge variety of characters remembered in it, and I have but touched the surface. This book is in memory of all these people, and I hope will be of interest to many.

I would like to give huge credit to the wonderful members of the choir who have come up through the years. It would not be possible to name them all, but Paul Jackson, Morris Parry, Richard Williams, Siân Dulfer, Robert Andrews and Wynn Davies come to mind, of recent times; Richard Williams should have a special mention as events manager and the maintenance and carer of the Cathedral grounds. Despite illness, he has put in a huge amount of work which is very much appreciated by everybody. We should also applaud the intrepid three gardeners, Todi Wakefield, Brian Stockton and Colin Jones for their splendid work.

A special mention for all the dedicated junior choristers. We wish Stephen Power the director of music and his assistant Jon Pilgrim all the very best, having made an excellent start to their tenure of office.

There have also been many excellent deans and some marvellous workers, sidesmen and sacristans including Jan Roberts, who unfortunately has recently died. She was hugely dedicated to the cathedral and did a whole variety of jobs including the maintenance of the vestments. She was particularly expert at embroidery and her skills were unsurpassed. A great contributor in the past was Mr Tilley, a verger who did much for the cathedral and who was instrumental in creating the lychgate. Other memorable stewards or wardens were June Jones and John Greatorex who were great servants of the cathedral. They have been replaced by two marvellous stewards, Rhiannon Lloyd and Colin Jones. We should mention Malcolm Johns a former great chorister and for a long time, captain of the belltower. Let us not forget Kelvin Redford, a great organist and musician.

Also, we shall never forget the hospitality and sheer joy of Dean Geoffrey Marshall and his wife Hazels welcoming regime.

We wish Dean Paul Shackerley and his splendid team of Residentiary Canon, Mark Clavier and Priest Vicar, Stephen Griffith all the very best for the future, and know how hard the Dean has worked to raise money for the cathedral.

It has been a privilege to worship there, and hopefully, many generations will continue to do so.

Lightning Source UK Ltd.
Milton Keynes UK
UKHW030238160821
388835UK00003B/5

9 781838 428938